"*Groaning in Labor, Growing in Hope* is a beautifully honest reflection on those early days of motherhood. While not shying away from the very brutal moments of challenge, the book extends a vision of hope that any parent would find solace in. Jessica Mannen Kimmet's prose unfolds her own conflicting memories of her maternal journey with love and candor. In addition to thoughtful scriptural reflections, the very practical invitations to prayer, suggestions of patron saints, and even the short chapter length extend a hand out of spiritual darkness. I would recommend this book to any new mother, knowing it would speak to her heart."

—Chelsea Piper Baldwin, Senior Coordinator
for Youth Ministry, Archdiocese of Chicago

"Jessica Mannen Kimmet speaks into the experience of postpartum depression and mental illness with gentleness and courage. Inviting readers to encounter through Scripture the loving presence of God, her reflections penetrate the isolation and shame that accompany so many women's experiences of motherhood. In a spirit of friendship, she encourages readers' faith in the loving presence of God who draws near to us, especially in those seasons when we feel most alone and despairing."

—Beth Hlabse, LMHCA, Director, Fiat Program on Faith
and Mental Health, McGrath Institute for Church Life,
University of Notre Dame

Groaning in Labor, Growing in Hope

Scripture Reflections for the Hard Days of Early Motherhood

Jessica Mannen Kimmet

LITURGICAL PRESS

Collegeville, Minnesota

www.litpress.org

1   2   3   4   5   6   7   8   9

Library of Congress Cataloging-in-Publication Data

Names: Kimmet, Jessica Mannen, author.
Title: Groaning in labor, growing in hope : scripture reflections for the
    hard days of early motherhood / Jessica Mannen Kimmet.
Description: Collegeville, Minnesota : Liturgical Press, [2023] |
    Summary: "In Groaning in Labor, Growing in Hope, Jessica Mannen
    Kimmet, a mom of three, offers a collection of Scripture readings
    and reflections that speak to the challenges of transitioning to
    motherhood. This resource includes lectio divina for moms, Scripture
    references for overwhelming times, a litany of Saints for postpartum
    struggles, and more"— Provided by publisher.
Identifiers: LCCN 2023009324 (print) | LCCN 2023009325 (ebook) |
    ISBN 9780814669167 (paperback) | ISBN 9780814669174 (epub) |
    ISBN 9780814669174 (pdf)
Subjects: LCSH: Mothers—Prayers and devotions. | Motherhood—
    Religious aspects—Christianity—Meditations.
Classification: LCC BV4847 .K56 2023 (print) | LCC BV4847 (ebook) |
    DDC 242/.6431—dc23/eng/20230510
LC record available at https://lccn.loc.gov/2023009324
LC ebook record available at https://lccn.loc.gov/2023009325

Contents

Acknowledgments   vii

Introduction   1

Part I: Seeds of Healing   9

Chapter 1: Groaning in Labor (Rom 8:22-24a)   11

Chapter 2: A New Heart (Ezek 36:26-27)   16

Chapter 3: Wait for God (Ps 42:6)   22

Part II: Companions in the Sorrow   27

Chapter 4: All She Had (Mark 12:42-44)   29

Chapter 5: Woman, Why Are You Weeping?
(John 20:15-16)   34

Chapter 6: A Sword Will Pierce (Luke 2:33-35)   38

Chapter 7: Take the Child and His Mother
(Matt 2:13-15)   44

Part III: Practical Strategies   49

Chapter 8: Everything That Has Breath
(Ps 150:6)   51

Chapter 9: Wonderfully Made (Ps 139:13-14)   57

Chapter 10: Speak to the Earth (Job 12:7-10)   63

Chapter 11: Give You Rest (Matt 11:28-30)   67

Closing Benediction: All Things New
                     (Rev 21:3-5a)   71

Appendix   75

A. *Lectio Divina* for Moms   75

B. Briefer Scriptures for Overwhelming Times   77

C. A Litany of Saints for Postpartum Struggles   79

D. Other Resources   85

Acknowledgments

Like all worthwhile projects, this book is the result of efforts that far exceed mine. I am so grateful for the support of John Kyler, who has been a hugely encouraging editor and friend, and the entire team at Liturgical Press. A special word of thanks goes to Monica Bokinskie, whose cover design brought me to tears.

I am enormously grateful to the writing group that Kassie Iwinski formed of internet friends in the midst of the COVID-19 pandemic. After the discouraging challenges of raising small humans in near isolation, this group offered much-needed companionship and pulled this book back from the brink of landing forever in my pile of unfinished projects. Kassie, Catherine Ippolito, Caitlin Irish, Emily Kuper, Stefanie Lilly, Mallory Nygard, Laura Pittenger, Marie Trotter, and Megan Ulrich read and commented on early drafts of every page here. Their feedback and encouragement and friendship have been invaluable; I do not exaggerate when I say this book would not exist without them.

Thanks also to Lisa DeLorenzo, Ellen Koneck, and Carolyn Pirtle, all of whom read early versions of early chapters and made this book better with their suggestions. Carolyn also suggested the title that stuck through the rest of the writing and editing process.

Because I will undoubtedly miss someone, I won't try to name them all here, but I owe huge thanks to all the mom friends who have shown excitement at this idea. Your reassurance that I am not alone in my struggles as well as your conviction that this was a worthwhile effort mean more than I can say, and I hope you know who you are.

A heartfelt thanks to Nicole Nemeth, Elizabeth Schulte, and Abby Cousins, all of whom served as regular babysitters while I worked on this book. I am so grateful to have found people to whom I can entrust my children.

Speaking of whom: thanks to Martin Theodore, Lucas Gabriel, and Dominic Bessette for being who you are. You are the greatest gifts God's given me, and your presence reminds me daily of a God who is loving and life-giving and playful and *good*. If you ever read this book, I hope you understand that the pain motherhood brought me never made my love for you any less. I'm so grateful that we've found our way to a happier place, but even when it hurt the most, you were always, *always* worth it.

Finally, thank you to my husband Mark, who has been endlessly patient with my shortcomings and endlessly supportive of my conviction that this book should come to be. Thank you for seeing abundance where I see scarcity, and thank you for choosing me. I love you.

Introduction

He wouldn't stop talking about the laundry.

I stood in the back of the church, wiggly toddler in my arms, walking that ever-precarious balance between teaching my child to participate in Mass and keeping him from disturbing those in the pews around us. He was going through one of the many phases of child-rearing that no one had thought to warn me about. In this one, his favorite pastime was to grab fistfuls of my neck skin between his chubby fingers, and he pursued this goal relentlessly.

In the meantime, our freshly-ordained associate pastor stood at the ambo delivering what I'm sure was, on paper, a lovely homily. He was talking about the sanctifying power of love, and he pointed to moms as an example. Mothers take up so much for their children, shouldering never-ending errands and house-keeping tasks to keep their families happy and healthy, he said. They do laundry, and dishes, and laundry, and tidying, and more laundry (the laundry example was, for some reason, really sticking with him).

1

But moms take all this on, he said, out of love for their children. I think he talked his way into quoting Mother Teresa, who is credited as saying, "I have found the paradox, that if you love until it hurts, there can be no more hurt, only more love." If you love your child enough, he seemed to say, it doesn't hurt anymore. Moms give themselves over to mothering, and their love erases the hurt. My brain filled in the rest: if it's still hurting, you don't love your child enough.

In the meantime, my child had his literal fingernails dug into my literal neck skin, leaving me longing for the days when I had been blissfully unaware that I even had enough neck skin to grab. I loved my kid, but unsurprisingly, this truth did not cause his tiny razor fingernails to stop hurting.

And that was the least of my pain. Ten months prior, I had pushed a nine-pound human out of my body, which tore my perineum and left me with a web of scar tissue that made exercise uncomfortable and marital intimacy excruciating. I had yet to discover the healing power of pelvic floor physical therapy (I don't think I knew yet what a pelvic floor even was), and I thought this was part of the normal pain of bringing a child into the world.

My sacroiliac joint had been pulled out of place by the weight of pregnancy, and I was deeply naive about the kind of rehabilitation my body needed after birth. My efforts to "get my body back" mostly consisted of trying to go for the sort of quick jog that had been easy prior to pregnancy. And these efforts resulted in injury—I kept hurting my back, over and over again. I thought this, too, was just going to be my new normal.

And beyond the physical pains, my mental and emotional health was in shambles. My mental capacity was diminished. I'd always been proud of my patience for other people's children; I'd had a knack for staying earnestly enthusiastic for toddler conversation long after most other adults gave up on it. That patience was gone. I'd been known in my professional life for unflappability, meeting challenging situations head-on and coolly solving problems that seemed overwhelming for others. That problem-solving capacity was gone. I'd been persistent, always trusting I'd find my way through challenges; now I was ready to just give up.

I wasn't bonding with my baby the way I thought I should be. I often felt anger and resentment where I expected the overwhelming rush of love that everyone had promised. I was sure I'd made a mistake, that I had somehow been wrong my whole life about my desire for children and my very call to motherhood. This was all the more heartbreaking because I had discerned it so carefully; in the sometimes-painful waiting of my single years, I'd tried to stay open to the idea that God might be calling me elsewhere, and it just never fit. Ongoing prayer and spiritual direction had seemed to consistently confirm that my call to motherhood was real, not just self-manufactured or culturally conditioned.

I had wanted this baby so badly. I'd been so scared that my irregular cycles would mean my fertility would be compromised. I'd charted those cycles and consulted multiple doctors and given up sugar and taken hormone supplements. I'd prayed, prayed hard, that my marriage would be blessed with children. When our first year of marriage had been nearing its end, my husband and I had traveled to Lourdes to pray for this intention, and we'd found out we were pregnant one month later. I should have felt nothing but gratitude and wonder toward the tiny blessing in my arms. The guilt at feeling anything else was overwhelming.

In hindsight, I see many signs in myself that were consistent with a diagnosis of postpartum depression, with which I would be formally diagnosed after my second child was born. After the first, though, I thought this was standard, just what life was like now that I was a mom. I thought I'd be in this physical and mental pain forever.

And this man would not stop talking about the laundry.

Look, the laundry can get tedious; maybe for you it is a particular burden. But for me, the idea that the tedium of the laundry was the worst of it was simply laughable—or it would have been laughable if feeling so unseen didn't leave me feeling like I was irreparably broken. Reducing the pain and sacrifice of motherhood to the tasks of motherhood feels reductionistic to me. There is so much more to it.

I bring up this homily because I think it represents well the disconnect I have often felt between what the church has taught me about motherhood and my own lived experience of it. This is a church that (rightly!) affirms the goodness of children and the sacredness of mothering. As a young adult, I was eager for motherhood, impatiently counting down the days until I met my husband, we married, and we started trying to have a baby. I expected this to be the pinnacle of my life, the most love I would ever hold, the closest I would ever get to God as I participated in God's life-giving nature.

Maybe it was all that. But it also hurt. A lot. And because no one told me how much it would hurt, I became convinced that there was something wrong with me.

After my second baby, I started learning how to better rehabilitate my physical self after pregnancy, but the emotional pain raged on. My patience was thin, my temper was short, and my poor toddler bore the brunt of this reality. My irritability would turn to anger that would turn to yelling that would turn to guilt that would turn to crying. It was hard crying, the kind that could derail whole days as I dragged myself through the minimum required to take care of two young children.

I finally admitted to myself that this didn't seem normal. I talked to my obstetrician and started a hormone supplement that helped me break out of the cyclical thinking I was stuck in. A few months later, I started therapy, and I made further progress in managing my responses to the normal challenges of parenthood. As a person of faith, I also sought out prayer resources for this new, complicated, confusing reality. My search came up surprisingly short. A few scattered blog posts were helpful, but that was really all there was.

The church can, I believe, do better. So as I continued to recover, I decided to write the book I wished I'd had. It is a common marker of all sorts of mental health issues to feel adrift from those things that should be anchors, so it is okay if faith and prayer feel like a struggle for you at this time. But if you'll let me, I'd love to walk with you through it. I am, I think, safely on the other side, but I'm still bruised and scarred and trying to make sense of the reality of those early years of mothering.

While a number of prayer practices supported my recovery, my greatest gifts from God came from reading Scripture, so that's what I've focused on here. The church teaches that Scripture is the living Word of God. God's voice is not just statically imprinted on the page but dynamically speaks into our real, actual lives. God is present not just in the writing of the Word thousands of years ago but also in the reading and receiving of the Word here and now.

So we'll read passages of Scripture together and listen for the way God might speak into the specific experience of early motherhood being hard. Like most women's experiences, the Bible doesn't talk a lot about this season specifically, but its stories of hurt and hope and healing have something to say to us. In Part I, we'll look at some passages that might help us begin to reframe our pain and maybe feel a little less lost in it. Part II will look at biblical companions who might have something to offer to our own journeys of healing. In Part III, I'll say a few words about some practical strategies, practices that have helped me survive the cluster of things that makes life as a new mom hard—and have helped me see those things as invitations from God.

I've tried to keep these chapters short; I hope it will work for you to read one during a single feeding session or whatever scrap of time you might be able to grab for yourself. But I know—I *know*—that even a short reflection is too much some days. So each chapter also ends with a very brief "prayer to carry." These prayers of less than twenty words are meant to be taken with you in a season where you likely cannot sit and pray for long amid your very busy day. In Appendix B, you'll also find shorter snippets from the Scripture passages we consider together. Please take these short offerings as a gift and use them however they might be helpful. Write them in your planner or stick them to your mirror. Chant them in the car or sing them in the shower. Whatever you need, wherever it fits, is the right way to do this.

An important note: if you suspect you are suffering from postpartum depression or anxiety, please do not attempt to use this book, or any form of prayer, to replace medical and psychological support. God can, of course, heal mental illness. But God very often works through our human reason and resources, including the care of professionals. My own recovery was supported by prayer, and it was also supported by my family doctor, my obstetrician, and a therapist. Prayer doesn't substitute for mental health care; it plays a different role, and you cannot pray your way out of needing counseling, medication, or both. If you need such support, please contact your doctor, or turn to Appendix D in the back of this book for some starting points in seeking out further care.

Finally, please remember that your prayer—or whatever attempt you can make right now—is valid whether or not it feels that way. You've opened this book, and that is already a very good start. You've shown up, and whether or not it stirs something in you is subject to a complex and unpredictable set of factors. Prayer is not always about feeling it; our feelings are fickle and human, and God is not. This is a time to practice love as a virtue, which keeps showing up even when love as an emotion fails us. You might not feel "in love" right now, with God or with your baby or with anything that used to stir those emotions in you. This time will test your love, but if you keep showing up, you will find—perhaps in ways you didn't expect—that God is always there waiting.

Part I

Seeds of Healing

Chapter 1

Groaning in Labor

"We know that all creation is groaning in labor pains even until now; and not only that, but we ourselves, who have the firstfruits of the Spirit, we also groan within ourselves as we wait for adoption, the redemption of our bodies. For in hope we were saved." (Rom 8:22-24a)

The birth of your baby: that was the easy part. What do you remember of labor now that you've been through it? My own memories are fuzzy; when specific glimpses emerge, I have to ask my husband if those particular moments really happened. But labor had a distinct beginning, even if it was unclear at the time. There was a first contraction or a breaking of water or the placement of a Foley bulb or a pre-op for a Cesarean. It had a distinct end, too, when the placenta passed to the outside of the body, an entire organ suddenly expendable, its job done. There was pain in between, plenty of it. There was deep exhaustion and, for me at least, my own voice hopelessly crying out that I couldn't do it. But the pain was mostly contained between the beginning and end of labor. And that pain had an unmistakable purpose. It was there to break my body open so that I could offer my baby to the world and the world to my baby. The payoff was pretty good.

Mothers need to be born, too, and the labor is less distinct, with blurry edges. You are a mom as soon as you get pregnant, before you're even aware of what's happening within you. You are a mom throughout your pregnancy, but we still speak of it in the future tense; "Mom to Be" banners adorn our baby showers. Your birth as a mother can be full of joy and hope, but it comes with pain, too, and the pain is spread out in a way that makes it feel less purposeful. We keep growing into this new identity as we shift, well, everything to make room for this new person in our bodies and our hearts and our world. There isn't necessarily a moment it's over, a moment when you know once and for all that you're a mom.

Some of this pain is universal to motherhood. And postpartum mood disorders bring another layer into it, robbing us more decisively of what is supposed to be a happy time. This is not necessary or right; postpartum depression and anxiety are signs of a world that has been broken by sin and evil. This is not how it is supposed to be. But whether you are experiencing an ordinary or an extraordinary kind of pain, I'm here to make the claim that this pain has a purpose, too, because Christ can take the pain and *make* it purposeful.

This text from Romans reveals the "already but not yet" dichotomy present in the Christian understanding of the world. Christ has already redeemed the world—"in hope we *were* saved" (Rom 8:24; emphasis added)—but the verses leading up to this passage reveal that we still wait with "eager expectation" for the fullness of that redemption (Rom 8:19). The saving work is done, but the effects of sin and death remain. The battle is won even as it rages on around us and within us.

Becoming a mother also comes with an "already but not yet" dynamic. You become a mother once and for all at the moment of conception. When God gave your baby a soul and gave the world an unspeakably precious, unrepeatable person, you, too, became a unique, unrepeatable mother to that little one. At the same time, though, you-as-mother are still becoming. There is much to learn: basic care skills like diaper changing and bathing, and bigger decisions like how sleep and discipline will best work for your unique family and how you'll interact with the wider community. And then there are the really big questions about who you are and what you bring to parenting. What did your own parents do well, and where could they have done better? Where will you intentionally depart from the familiar paths of how you were raised? How will your weaknesses curtail your baby's development? How will your strengths bolster them? This is a lot, and some of it hurts to consider, and when postpartum mood disorders are taking away your resilience and energy, it becomes a nearly unbearable process.

In the verses prior to this passage, St. Paul asserts that our sufferings are "as nothing" in comparison to what God has in store for us when our suffering is over (Rom 8:18). But it sure doesn't feel like nothing when you're going through it. Paul knew this—his fervent ministry was rewarded with persecution and imprisonment and, ultimately, martyrdom. And his pain, like yours and mine, was part of a birthing, part of how he fulfilled his mission of bringing the newness of Christ's story to the world. Through the uncertainty and pain he endured, life came forth.

We mothers also experience uncertainty and pain, participating in another kind of martyrdom. We make countless sacrifices, and even if we can't see how, these sacrifices clear space for God's creative power to do its work. When we bear a new soul into the world, we are making God's presence more evident. As we ourselves become mothers, we are witnessing to the unendingly creative love of God. But in the meantime, it hurts. What are we supposed to do with that?

Paul continues this passage with an important hint when he mentions that "we hope for what we do not see" (Rom 8:25). The early days of motherhood are *hard*, and the harsh realities often steal away what we hoped for from these days, but we can still strive for hope even when we do not see the goodness we thought motherhood would bring. We may not get the full experience of the warm and lovey feelings we were promised in our baby's first year, but we hope in something far greater and more real than our own emotions.

And there is hope. This doesn't last forever. I'm only six years into parenting, and I already look back at the acute phase of maternal growing pains as a brief blip in the family life that is continuing to unfold. Healing is coming, and as you wait for it to emerge, there's a beautiful dramatic tension in the anticipation. All creation is waiting with you as your groaning continues and as you labor to birth yourself as a mother. You are part of something bigger now, stepping in to find your place in the ongoing dance of birth and life and suffering and, yes, even joy.

*A **prayer to carry:** Jesus, take my pain and make it purposeful.*

Chapter 2

A New Heart

"I will give you a new heart, and a new spirit I will put within you. I will remove the heart of stone from your flesh and give you a heart of flesh. I will put my spirit within you so that you walk in my statutes, observe my ordinances, and keep them." (Ezek 36:26-27)

When I saw my first positive pregnancy test, I was surprised that I didn't feel more immediately joyful. I had struggled a bit to get pregnant—and had longed for marriage and motherhood for many years before that. I *wanted* this baby. I had made difficult diet changes and seen a doctor repeatedly and taken supplements religiously. I had prayed rosaries and novenas and had flown across an ocean to light a candle at Lourdes and be plunged into its freezing-cold waters. So while I wasn't surprised to be pregnant, my primary emotion was not the joy I had expected. It was, rather, an overpowering bewilderment.

And this feeling continued throughout my pregnancy. I constantly felt like I was falling short of the excitement I thought I was supposed to feel. Since I had wanted this so badly, I also felt *guilty* for these less-than-enthusiastic feelings. I wanted to be nothing but grateful and joyful.

I heard from others that this was not uncommon; after all, I hadn't even met my baby yet. Despite our unique physical proximity, it would be a total stranger who emerged from my body at the end of labor. I frequently heard that the moment he was placed in my arms would make up for it all. I was reassured over and over that when I first saw my baby's face, I would feel a rush of love like nothing I'd ever experienced.

I did not. There was no rush of anything. My baby was placed in my arms and remained an absolute stranger. I loved him, in a sense. I was ready to care for him and to set my needs aside in the process. But it was a sense of duty and of moral obligation and of stubborn determination to be a "good mom" that carried me where emotion did not.

Then came the anger. And the guilt. And the hopelessness. This mix of emotion would become a familiar characteristic of my first three years of parenting, but the night it first surfaced hit me particularly hard. My eldest was about three weeks old, still in that newborn stage where nights and days were mixed up, and he spent his early morning hours nursing and fussing and nursing again as I rocked and walked him for what felt like interminable stretches of time. On that particular night, he seemed to have finally settled, and I was just starting to finally drift to sleep when I heard him start fidgeting and whimpering again.

In that moment of bleary sleep deprivation and persistent pain from the tear I'd sustained during delivery, I was blindingly, overwhelmingly angry at him. I'm not proud to admit this, but the word "hate" even crossed my mind. I knew it wasn't true; it couldn't be true. I was known for being unflappable, for rolling with professional challenges and conquering potential overload through relentless organization. Having a temper had not been part of my adult disposition up to that point. But there I was, about to lose it. At the very one I'd prayed so long and hard for. At my most generous gift from God. At my poor, sweet newborn who just didn't know any better, who just wanted the warmth and comfort of his mama's arms. What on earth was wrong with me?

Those early days are rather blurry in my memory, but that moment stands out with startling clarity. The self-doubt it manifested would continue pretty unchecked for another three years or so. I doubted often whether I was supposed to be this child's mom, or a mom at all. I believed deeply in the importance and beauty of motherhood—moms are a beautiful and unique expression of God's unconditional love. But I was not that. I was impatient and cold and weirdly detached from the whole thing. It was so clear to me all the ways I was falling short.

I clung to small moments where I experienced flashes of what I thought I was supposed to feel. At four months, I watched him watch his first snow. He was wearing a blue-and-white-striped shirt that had a built-in hoodie attached, a couple curls of his dark hair were getting long across his forehead, and his eyes had lost their blue and were just settling into the greenish brown they'd become. My heart softened a bit, and for a moment I felt like I could be falling in love with him. At six months, I cheered him on as he army-crawled across the room. It was gray-and-white stripes that day, one-piece pajamas that left his feet bare so I could see his toes flex as he experimented with sitting and moving. He acquired the giraffe toy he'd been pursuing, I congratulated him heartily, and he delighted in my delight in him. I wondered at his growth, happening even when I felt like I was failing. And I thought we would be okay.

But his toddler years were very, very rough. He was strong-willed; I was exhausted. He thrived on intense individual attention; my introverted self struggled to keep up with his needs. He was active and daring and contrary, all of which *sounded* like the kind of child I wanted to raise, but the relentlessness of the everyday reality was wearing me out. I was irritable, and the irritability escalated to anger all too easily. When my second child was born, I suffered more clearly from postpartum depression and had more moments and days where I worried that anger and even hate were consuming me. My heart was scarred from the suffering. It felt old and tired and dry. And it felt like it was getting worse, crusted over with bitterness as I continued to judge myself a failure. I worried constantly about this stony heart that was somehow mine.

I had this idea that if I could learn to see Christ in my children, all would be well. I believed, in one sense, that Christ was there; he had taken on all of the human condition, including the dependence of small children, and anyway, my children's baptisms meant that they were incarnating him to the world in their own unique ways. But it was not natural for me to see him there. My usual imaginings of Jesus see him as an adult. He's someone who converses and heals. He's brave and loving and generous. He cares for others.

Seeing Christ in my children is learning to recognize him in disguise. And this is no small thing. Many saint stories involve an unrecognized Christ in a beggar; seeing Jesus in the ones who need our help is the work of literal saints. And our children come to us in all their neediness. They are weak and poor and vulnerable. They have no assets of their own or voice in society. Their utter dependence makes for a very different image of Christ than what I'm used to thinking of.

But it's an image that—slowly, uncertainly—is replacing my stony heart with a softer one. It doesn't always happen all at once or in ways that are obvious, but God does heal and renew our hearts. God is gradually, I think, giving me the kind of heart that I always thought moms were supposed to have. This is not some superhuman heart that never gets angry when I'm drowning in unseen labor or unmet needs. But it's a heart that bounces back, that returns to love with a firm resolve that might even be called stubbornness.

Hearts of flesh are hard to bear—they break and bleed more easily than stone—but they also heal. For me, learning to love like a mom didn't happen as naturally as I expected; it was instead a long, hard road. But all along, God was putting God's own heart within me. And God still is. This is a lifelong process; I'll never love my kids perfectly on this side of death. But God is slowly fulfilling the promise here, taking my heart and making it new and being with me, as my God, all the while.

A prayer to carry: *Creator God, make my heart anew.*

Chapter 3

Wait for God

"Why are you downcast, my soul;
   why do you groan within me?
Wait for God, for I shall again praise him,
   my savior and my God." (Ps 42:6)

"Why are you downcast, my soul?" Very often, the answer to that lies in unmet expectations.

Now, I'm not here to chide you for *having* expectations. The advice to "adjust your expectations" is all too common. When I started reading up on postpartum depression, this oft-repeated mantra felt like a mild scolding: *It's your fault that you feel this way. You were expecting the wrong things. You didn't prepare well enough. You didn't study hard enough, and now you're failing the test.* But having expectations is only human, and having expectations about motherhood is downright encouraged by our culture and by our church.

Heck, even the word "expecting" is synonymous with "pregnant." Throughout pregnancy and early mother-hood, we are treated to endless advice and anecdotes, and it would be unrealistic to expect us to wade through all that and come out with no expectations.

Particularly perfidious is the way our exposure to social media misshapes our expectations. The internet can be a huge gift to new moms, offering access to endless knowledge and the ability to connect with others in what is a notoriously isolating time. But this phenomenon is still pretty new, and we're still discovering all the ramifications of our constant connectedness for our minds and hearts. One thing that's clear, though, is that self-esteem is suffering as we live with the ceaseless presence of other people's highlight reels and the natural temptation to compare them to the complications of our own lives.

I often find inspiration and edification in following Catholic mom accounts, but these come with their own set of dangers, particularly tricky because they come clothed in the language of faith. It's a good thing that there are people out there showing the beauty hidden in this life that is often so hard. But some of these folks have made a mission out of—and, in some cases, are even making a living off—putting their highlights in front of my face. They may post religiously-inspired content, but their perfect lighting and unattainably expensive kitchens make them look more marketing campaign than ministry. And marketing works precisely by making us feel less than whole. It aims to convince us that we are somehow inferior if we don't use this product or subscribe to this service. The underlying message of nearly all marketing is that we are not good enough.

When this message is clad in religious language, it's particularly insidious. The "not enough" becomes about core pieces of our identity and can make us question our goodness as mothers, as people, and even as daughters of God. Women who are particularly gifted decorators and photographers seem to go about the work of motherhood in a way that makes actual, visible beauty flow into their homes and out onto our screens. It is at least implied, and sometimes explicitly claimed, that the aesthetic they have achieved is the fruit of their faith and their gracious acceptance of motherhood's sacrifices.

But our sincerity of heart and the strength of our faith are not actually attached to our lives *looking* a certain way. The beauty God calls us to is not necessarily photogenic and does not necessarily fit any particular aesthetic. And for me, at least, much of this online content had formed (and misformed) my expectations for motherhood. I was eager to pour myself out in the diligent daily sacrifices that would unite me to Christ on the cross. And I expected it to be beautiful along the way.

But motherhood is also painful in ways that don't show up on social media and in ways I utterly failed to expect. It has nearly broken me with the physical and mental pain it brought. I've been faced with my own failings daily, as motherhood has exposed unseen pockets of selfishness and expectations that I was imposing without realizing or questioning. I've questioned daily if I am doing a good enough job. I've wondered, often, if someone else would have made a better mother for my children. In my darkest moments, I've wondered if someone else still could. Where the work of mothering was ostensibly making the Catholic mom influencers' hearts blossom in beauty, my own heart was feeling increasingly old and tired and crusty.

But no. God gave these babies to me and me to them. I don't always understand why, but I can try to trust that God did so on purpose. I can seek to retrain my eyes to see the beauty present in my struggles, even though it is not as visible as the beauty that saturates my various social media feeds. I can remind myself that the cross is beautiful only because it is not the whole story. Resurrection is hidden within it, sometimes really deeply hidden, but there nonetheless.

And here is where expectations can serve us well: when we place our trust in God. God alone deserves our trust, even when God's timelines and plans for our lives do not match what we have come to envision. Like the psalmist, we can instruct our souls to wait for God, anticipating that God will fulfill all God's promises in time.

When I was first introduced to the practice of centering prayer, I learned to choose a word to focus on, a touchstone to bring my thoughts back when they wandered. I chose the word "still." I meant it in the sense of calm or silent, as in "Be still and know that I am God" (Ps 46:11). When I use this word in my prayer now, it speaks of endurance, of still being here, of still choosing hope. Some translations of Psalm 42:6 use it in this sense: "I will praise him still."

The psalmist recognizes that praise is a choice. It is nice when it pours forth spontaneously from emotive love and gratitude, but very often it arises from stubborn refusal to let go of God even when pain remains. So we can choose praise even when we don't feel it. And in doing so, we choose hope, the virtuous form of expectation that never lets us down. In hope, we take in the images of our real lives and choose to seek God there—and God promises to be there for us to find.

A prayer to carry: God, give me patience to wait for you.

Part II

Companions
in the Sorrow

Chapter 4

All She Had

"A poor widow also came and put in two small coins worth a few cents. Calling his disciples to himself, [Jesus] said to them, 'Amen, I say to you, this poor widow put in more than all the other contributors to the treasury. For they have all contributed from their surplus wealth, but she, from her poverty, has contributed all she had, her whole livelihood.'" (Mark 12:42-44)

One thing I didn't prepare for was how motherhood would change the way I pray. In my life before kids, I loved to pray the Liturgy of the Hours. I delighted in the intricacies of setting up my ribbons and relished the rich language of the Psalms. But in those early, overwhelming moments of motherhood, my books were out of reach, and my movement was hampered by a baby I desperately wanted to keep asleep. I had to pray with whatever I could find within myself. And

it was, almost to my surprise, "Hail Mary, full of grace
. . ." The Hail Mary had not been one of the standbys
in my adult prayer up to that point. It had felt almost
too basic, a prayer of my childhood, committed to
memory many years ago. But it was written deeply
onto my heart by decades of repetition, and when I
didn't have much to offer, it became everything I had.
I would throw it up in desperation, repeat it over and
over, and wish that I could do more.

When I later reflected on this shift in my prayer, the
widow offering her two coins came to mind. This is an
image my husband and I adopted early in our marriage
as a bit of a family emblem; the idea of offering our
little bit, even when it seems not enough, has encouraged us through a lot of tough times. We once bought,
and now have framed, a real Roman coin of the sort
the widow would have offered, sometimes called a
"mite." It is tiny. It is hard to see, and it would be easy
to ignore. It's really not much of anything at all. But
two of these tiny mites were all this woman had.

While the widow's moment in Scripture is brief, I
have come to think of her as one of my biblical companions. I wonder often about how she felt as she
offered the little she did. Was she embarrassed at her
gift's smallness? Proud of her generosity? Or just sat-
isfied that she had done the best she could? Did she
overhear Jesus's words? Or was she distracted by the
larger gifts being made?

In some ways, it doesn't matter. The important thing about this woman is that she shows up and gives what she can. And we can, too. Motherhood changes us; it breaks us apart. We have done an amazing thing, but it was not without cost. We have been physically split open, and our bodies are left stretched, weakened, softened. Our attention is fractured. Our time is relentlessly interruptible. Even thoughts go unfinished. We can't offer what we once could.

Even in the best and most privileged situations, becoming a mom takes everything we have. Pregnancy stretches the literal boundaries of our bodies as our bodies make space for an entire other person. And that's just a shadow of what happens to our minds and hearts and spirits. Walls are knocked down; new spaces are made. Naomi Stadlen talks about this phenomenon in her book *What Mothers Do: Especially When It Looks Like Nothing*. She calls it the process of making space and makes the case that, despite its invisibility, it deserves more credit as real work (or at least a name so that we can talk about it more easily). Because everything about us is affected—everything we have, everything we think, everything we are. Just everything.

In the year after I was formally diagnosed with postpartum depression, I felt the weight of this. I didn't have much time or much energy. Even just in daily life, I didn't "succeed" at much of what I "should" have been doing. I bought an embarrassing amount of premade convenience food, and my toddler watched an embarrassing amount of TV. I wasn't able to find the energy to take good care of myself, and I certainly didn't feel I had much to offer to God. An occasional Hail Mary was about what I could muster.

I got lucky, though, because God offered me assurance that my efforts, however small and meaningless they might have seemed, were seen and loved. I was on a moms' retreat that welcomed breastfeeding infants to accompany their mothers. My second was breastfeeding but was about the oldest child in attendance—at ten months, he was starting to toddle and was not content to rest in my arms for very long. So the retreat wasn't really much of a break. My attention was splintered as I supervised him, and I only heard fragments of each talk as I paced around the back of meeting spaces, willing him to maintain some semblance of his nap schedule in that unfamiliar place.

But the heart of the retreat was all-night adoration, with groups invited to spend a quiet nighttime hour in prayer before the Blessed Sacrament. During my hour, I sat in the back, snuggling my baby to try to keep him quiet and still, mostly failing to focus on my prayer and on Jesus's presence. Adoration has never really been my favorite way to pray. I know that Jesus is present there and that I can never deserve the gift of that presence, and I am often grateful. But that's it—just a quiet, trusting being-together. But on that night, even as I felt my failure to really be there, I was gifted with an overwhelming sense that Jesus *loved* that I was there. I was sure, at least for a moment, that the God who gives me everything and to whom I can give not much of anything at all *loved* my faltering, flailing attempts to be closer to him.

All I had to do was show up. I put my two mites in, and God was there waiting, with strength beyond imagining and love beyond telling.

God doesn't always give us such clear reassurances; they are a gift when they come, but we very often need to muddle through without them. But God is no less present when we don't feel them. God is present to our smallness and to all the ways motherhood breaks us open. God can take what we have to offer, and God can make it meaningful. God can heal our brokenness and make us whole again.

Maybe everything you can offer seems small right now. Maybe what you have for God is just making it to weekly Mass; maybe it's short, memorized, repetitive prayer; maybe it's conversational prayer that is more bewilderedly angry than gratefully loving. Whatever it is, keep bringing it. Keep showing up. Jesus knows it's everything you have. And he loves you for it.

A prayer to carry: Jesus, help me keep showing up.

Chapter 5

Woman, Why Are You Weeping?

"Jesus said to her, 'Woman, why are you weeping? Whom are you looking for?' She thought it was the gardener and said to him, 'Sir, if you carried him away, tell me where you laid him, and I will take him.' Jesus said to her, 'Mary!' She turned and said to him in Hebrew, 'Rabbouni,' which means Teacher." (John 20:15-16)

I always find my prayer life disrupted during major life transitions; a wise spiritual director once reassured me that this is normal. Prayer, because it invites rather than demands our attention, is very often among the last things to settle in when everything has been upended. As I began to recover from postpartum depression, it just so happened that I returned to my regular practice of praying morning prayer from the Liturgy of the Hours on the feast of St. Mary Magdalene. She's long been one of my favorite saints, a courageous witness to the crucifixion and resurrection, the first to preach the very best of all good news. We don't know whether she was a mother—if she was, that aspect of her identity has been lost to history and is not part of the story we continue to tell—so I was not expecting her, this utter gift of a saint, to become such a powerful companion for my mothering journey. But on her feast day, her story reached through the maternal darkness I'd been struggling with and gently began to lift my eyes back to Christ.

The antiphons for this feast day's morning prayer summarize Mary's experience of encountering Christ at the tomb. In three small bits of Scripture, we hear the story of her exchange with Jesus and her emotional arc, passing from sorrow to confusion to recognition. The face-to-face interaction with Jesus at the tomb is a moment unique to Mary Magdalene, but the experience of encounter is one we might share in.

The first antiphon poses a question: "Jesus said to Mary: Woman, why are you weeping? Whom do you seek?" (John 20:15). Postpartum depression meant that I'd been crying a lot, mostly in secret moments when I could hide even from my kids. Here, Mary is weeping, too, catching a private moment of grief at the tomb of her beloved dead. I am not alone in my tears, in my feelings of loss and of not knowing where to go next. And what's more, I am not alone in being seen. For Jesus *sees* Mary here. He sees her tears, and he acknowledges them. He is not afraid of her show of emotion but meets it, encountering her right where she is. Jesus sees our tears, too; his love is big enough to receive us even when we do not come to him in joy.

The second antiphon quotes Mary Magdalene herself: "They have taken my Lord away, and I do not know where they have put him" (John 20:13). There's a wonderful irony to this line, spoken to the face of the very Lord she is seeking. We can imagine his slight smile at her lack of recognition, a surprise from one who knew him so well. For me too, though, depression makes it hard to recognize Christ in the once-reliable places. The sacraments feel dry, and it takes an enormous act of will to trust that they still are what I believe they are. I feel isolated in relationships, tempted to believe that I'm alone in my struggles and that no one understands what I'm going through. It can feel like postpartum depression has taken my Lord away, and I do not know where to look to regain the intimate and joyful relationship I once had with God.

And then there's the final antiphon, where Jesus and Mary finally come into dialogue with each other: "Jesus said: Mary. She turned to him and said: Rabboni, which means teacher" (John 20:16). Jesus says just one word: her name. I can't always remember the last time I've heard my name. The calls for "Mama" are endless, threatening to erase my identity as anything other than milk-maker and snack-retriever and Netflix-starter. But God knows my name and continues to call it, seeing me in all my fullness, as nothing more or less than beloved daughter. God sees all the hiddenness and smallness of this life, and God loves me no less for it.

So I try to join Mary Magdalene in her response. She calls Christ her teacher, returning to a state of trust even after her heart has been broken by following him. As I've joined Mary Magdalene in her tears and weeping, in her struggle to see Christ, I also strive to join her in her moment of discovery, when she recognizes the one she's been seeking is here with her after all. I try to turn back to knowing my identity rests in God. I try to let Christ teach me that he's still here, right here with me, whether I recognize him or not.

A prayer to carry: Jesus, see me in my weeping.

Chapter 6

A Sword Will Pierce

"The child's father and mother were amazed at what was said about him; and Simeon blessed them and said to Mary his mother, 'Behold, this child is destined for the fall and rise of many in Israel, and to be a sign that will be contradicted (and you yourself a sword will pierce) so that the thoughts of many hearts may be revealed.'" (Luke 2:33-35)

In my garden blooms a cluster of bleeding hearts. These are curiously-shaped flowers, with just four odd petals. The two on the outside form the heart shape for which the plant is named, and they curl slightly outward to reveal the two inner petals hanging below the heart in the shape of a teardrop—or, perhaps, a drop of blood emerging from the heart; this is certainly what the namer of these flowers envisioned. Legends abound about the origin of this flower, usually connecting it to the heartbreak of unrequited love. In some Catholic circles, though, it has been reclaimed as a symbol of Mary's pierced heart, and it is this meaning that I intend in my own garden.

Mary goes by many titles, including "Our Lady of Sorrows" and "Sorrowful Mother." Mary knows deep pain; throughout her life, she lost her plans and her home and her child. When I was suffering from postpartum depression, I realized that I, too, could claim this title of sorrowful mother. I was sad, I was a mother, and my sorrow was tied up in my motherhood in ways that were bewildering. So much in our culture and in our church tells us that mothers aren't supposed to be sorrowful. Having a baby is supposed to be the happiest time in your life, the fulfillment of your feminine identity. So we keep these sorrows hidden, perhaps at most whispering them to a trusted friend or family member. But we who struggle through motherhood are not alone. For Mary, too, motherhood was tied up in pain. She became pregnant before she was married, bravely allowing her reputation and marriage to be put on the line. And from then on, motherhood unfolded in a way she could not have imagined and probably would not have chosen for herself.

For much of the church's history, imaginations have been captured by the idea of weeping with Mary in her sorrow. Joining our tears with hers inspired the famous "Stabat Mater" hymn that we sing during

Stations of the Cross. And images of the sorrowing Mary are bountiful. When depicting this title, art often shows Mary with swords piercing her heart, an image gleaned from Simeon's prophecy in the temple. As far as we know, a sword never literally pierced Mary, so this prophecy has come to be understood as predicting the sorrows that would wound her throughout her motherhood. Devotees to the Sorrowful Mother have traditionally named seven scriptural moments as the seven sorrows.

The first three of Mary's sorrowful moments occur during the childhood of Jesus and are thus, I think, particularly relatable for the struggles of new motherhood. First, we have Simeon's chilling prophecy itself, which, when we stop to think about it, reminds us of the strangeness of Mary's motherhood. We know in hindsight that this was a figurative sword that would pierce her and that ample joy would be there to counterbalance it. But her knowledge of Jesus's mission and her own part in it came in mysterious pieces, never a complete road map. Like all of us, she faced uncertainty about who her child would be and what that would mean for her. She knew better than any of us that God was holding her through the uncertainty, but she still would have experienced the uncertainty in its fullness.

Then there was the flight into Egypt, when a viciously jealous ruler threatened Mary's new baby, and her little family fled in the night to a foreign place to keep him safe. This scene is terrifying beyond words. When my first baby was born, I could barely walk to the car, yet there was Mary, climbing back onto a donkey for a long, rough ride to a strange place. Gone were her support systems, the network of family and friends and small village connections that she would have been counting on. Instead, she had to navigate the newness of motherhood in a new land. That was not what she'd expected. That was not what motherhood was supposed to be. She'd already had to adjust her plans, yet there she was, forced to remake them again.

And then there was the loss of the child Jesus in the temple due to a relatable human miscommunication about which parent he should have been with. This moment captures much of the weight of parenthood: this parenting blunder was a genuine mistake, with no sin attached, but still had very scary potential consequences. Can you imagine the guilt and fear that Mary would have felt as she searched? The terror of *losing* this miracle baby that had been entrusted to her care? There were no phones to text, no Amber Alerts to be issued. It all turned out well in the end, but for *three days* Mary and Joseph looked for him, having no guarantee that he was anywhere they would think to look. There was no guarantee he was safe at all.

After Jesus was lost and found, he returned with Mary and Joseph to Nazareth, and his growing up continued, by all accounts, uneventfully. Mary, though, "kept all these things in her heart" (Luke 2:51). Luke repeats this refrain twice in his second chapter. It is initially a response of joy; Mary ponders the praise and words of the shepherds who appear out of nowhere to praise her baby boy and affirm his identity as Savior and Messiah (Luke 2:19). But here, it sums up her response to the *entire* infancy narrative, with all its joys and with all its bewilderment and in all its sorrows. Tradition has it that Luke knew Mary in her old age and received his version of the infancy narratives directly from her, which is why we get these little glimpses into her heart—only she could have told him what was going on there.

And perhaps it is in this pondering that Mary gives us one model for what to do with our pain. She held her pain, sat with it, waited with it. She wondered what it meant. She didn't forget it or suppress it; it was still accessible to her years later as she passed her story on to St. Luke. She absorbed the pain somehow, letting it transform her. It enabled her to make space for the pain of others and to stand more firmly in solidarity with all who suffer, including us. Mary has left all earthly pain behind her, but she still chooses to be with us in ours. She is able to weep with us because she has known the very real pains of motherhood.

Meditating on Mary as the Sorrowful Mother gave me a wonderful companion throughout my experience with postpartum depression. But it's important to note that this is not all there is of her. She is also Queen of Heaven, raised body and soul to be the first to share fully in Christ's resurrection. Her sorrow, born of immense love, was transformed to joy. She remains a companion in our own sorrow while also inviting us to the other side.

And so, the year after I recovered from postpartum depression, I dug into the cool autumn dirt near my garden's statue of Mary and placed bare roots, twisted tubers that looked like nothing. The next spring, ferny green foliage emerged, followed by strings of heart-shaped blossoms with a teardrop shape emerging from the bottom. Gardens are replete with resurrection imagery. Seeds that are not evidently living things somehow send out shoots and greenery. Barrenness transforms into fertility, bareness into beauty. Nature cycles through life and death and rising again, over and over. For me, the bleeding hearts in my garden serve as a reminder of the painful season of postpartum depression and of Mary's companionship through it and all the seasons of motherhood yet to come.

A prayer to carry: *God, transform my sorrow to joy.*

Chapter 7

Take the Child and His Mother

"When [the magi] had departed, behold, the angel of the Lord appeared to Joseph in a dream and said, 'Rise, take the child and his mother, flee to Egypt, and stay there until I tell you. Herod is going to search for the child to destroy him.' Joseph rose and took the child and his mother by night and departed for Egypt. He stayed there until the death of Herod, that what the Lord had said through the prophet might be fulfilled, 'Out of Egypt I called my son.'" (Matt 2:13-15)

In the previous chapter, we reflected on the image of Mary as Sorrowful Mother. One of her traditional sorrows—the flight into Egypt—deserves a chapter of its own. Art often depicts this scene idyllically, showing the Holy Family at some restful waypoint after they can be sure they're safe. But having gone through three real-life postpartum phases, I read the story of the flight into Egypt with absolute horror. Mary has to do *what?* She already consented to a plan that entirely uprooted her life, nearly cost her marriage, and subjected her to all sorts of gossip. She gave birth not at home surrounded by female relatives but in a smelly stable surrounded by animals. This has been tough. But it's not over yet.

Now, some church fathers held that Mary's labor was painless, that her sinlessness meant she did not share the pains of childbirth that had been given to Eve as punishment for her disobedience. I'm not sure I buy that—Christ himself, after all, was not spared from death, the ultimate price of sin—but even if we let them have it, a childbirth without *pain* does not translate to a childbirth without *any* effect. Lochia still would have run as the wound from her detached placenta slowly healed. Her breasts would have leaked as her body learned to produce milk to match her baby's needs. Even if it somehow weren't painful, she would have been swollen in unmentionable places that had stretched to let Jesus into the light. Like all of ours, her body would have needed time to heal.

It's not entirely clear how much time Mary had to heal before being whisked to Egypt. Luke holds that she visited the temple in Jerusalem forty days after Jesus's birth and returned home to Nazareth after.

Matthew has her still in Bethlehem when the magi visit, and the Holy Family departs for Egypt directly from there. However these accounts fit together, this seems like an *awful lot* of travel by donkey for a new mother to endure. Her packing would have been hurried; she may have had only what she'd brought to Bethlehem, leaving behind the belongings that bring comfort to a home.

Worst of all, this is entirely non-optional. This is not an idealistic move for a better job opportunity for Joseph or a relocation to be closer to family support. This is a life-and-death situation, the stuff of absolute nightmares. There is a political leader out to murder Mary's newborn baby. She never would have chosen this scenario. No one would have chosen this.

The biblical account only gives three verses to this total upheaval of Mary's life, and Matthew's infancy narratives focus more on Joseph's perspective than on Mary's. She feels a bit different from Luke's Mary of the courageous *fiat* and the daring *Magnificat* and the curious pondering. Matthew's Mary is a more passive recipient of Joseph's suspicion and the magi's visit and Herod's horrors. And in this, there is some powerful solidarity for those of us who suffer after the birth of a child. In this gospel, motherhood is something that happens *to* Mary—a feeling many of us can relate to. She is tugged around by forces outside her, heart-wrenchingly distant from whatever plans she had laid for her life. For Mary, as for many of us, motherhood was not what she expected.

It wasn't supposed to be like this, Mary might have thought as her family fled to Egypt. *It wasn't supposed to be like this*, I thought as I daily broke down weeping at my perceived failure at motherhood.

The comparison feels a little pathetic; the struggles I experienced in my extremely privileged life are, of course, nothing like what Mary had to endure. But she *knows* suffering in motherhood. She knows this does not always go the way we thought it would. And she, with heavenly compassion we cannot comprehend, sits with us in our struggles, too, easy as they might seem by comparison.

She also gives us a model of how to suffer well. She suffers well because she trusts that God is present even when evidence points to the contrary. Mary had angels and stars and mysterious foreign visitors to affirm that what she was doing was out of the ordinary, and maybe those things gave her some consolation. But the Bible only gives us these few extraordinary snippets from her life—the rest was filled with regular rhythms very much like ours, where it is harder to see God at work.

I have to imagine that, even for Mary, life with a baby got painfully tedious and mind-numbingly boring. We don't know much about how she responded to these challenges. How she expressed herself within the context of her family life is rather a mystery. We don't know much about how Mary talked to Jesus, what kind of attention she gave him, how she taught him all he needed to know.

Here's what we do know: we know she had this habit of pondering things in her heart, letting herself feel them and letting them shape her. Maybe we can imitate that, taking time to notice our own feelings and to reflect on what they're telling us about God and ourselves and the new ways we're called to be in the world. We know Mary acted out of love uninterrupted by sin. We can't imitate this perfectly, of course, but we can strive to always do a little better tomorrow, trying to replace a little more irritation with patience and a little more anger with love. And we know that Mary listened for God, who appeared to her not only in heavenly visitors but in the struggles of her motherhood. We can imitate that, too, trusting that God is with us as God was with her, in our sorrows and struggles, both the everyday and the extraordinary.

A prayer to carry: God, help me suffer well.

Part III

Practical Strategies

Chapter 8

Everything That Has Breath

"Let everything that has breath
   give praise to the LORD!
Hallelujah!" (Ps 150:6)

Psalm 150 is the final song in the book of Psalms. This book brings us through the vast range of human emotion and finds God in all of it. It ends with a rich outpouring of praise, calling us to bring all we have and all we are into worship of God. This final psalm culminates by calling on creation—"everything that has breath" (Ps 150:6)—to join in our praise before it falls into silence. This is a fascinating way to name us and our fellow creatures: by the breaths we take.

When I finally brought myself to see a therapist for my postpartum struggles, the first thing she did was remind me to use my breath to my advantage. She correctly and compassionately identified the anger I'd been feeling as a stress response, and she helped me realize that one of the biggest changes I needed to make was to manage my stress proactively. In life before kids, it had always been enough to work on stress *reactively*, as the stressors came. I could take a step away from whatever was causing stress, figure out a plan, and return better able to address the problem. But now, I often wasn't able to step away from my children the way I'd been able to step away from my desk. Plus, stressors were a given. It wasn't unkind to assume that stress was coming in a day with small people; it was a survival strategy. I could wait until the stress had overtaken me, or I could start managing it before it was noticeable. To do this, I had to make a discipline of stress relief, and that included working breathing exercises into my day.

We made a plan for when, where, and how often I'd incorporate these breathing exercises, and I honestly walked out of that therapy session rolling my eyes just a little. I *know* how to breathe. I know how to breathe *well*; a lifetime in choirs taught me that. I even know how to breathe in prayerful, meditative ways; I'd been on enough retreats to understand the physical benefits and how it could connect to emotional and spiritual ones as well. Surely I didn't just spend a very expensive hour being reminded to do the very first thing a baby does after birth.

But it *worked*. Making time to notice my breath and to breathe slowly and deeply made a significant, noticeable difference to my days.

Great, you're thinking, *another thing I should be doing right now*. I know. But the physiological effects of breathing deeply, slowly, and carefully are hard to deny. Diaphragmatic breathing reduces heart rate and stress hormones and blood pressure and even pain. And you need to breathe anyway; you might as well make it work for you a little bit.

You've probably encountered some instruction on the sort of breathing I mean—it abounds in various exercise techniques and wellness practices and prayer opportunities—so you may already know what I'm talking about and have a technique that works for you. But in case you don't, here's a quick primer on deep, diaphragmatic breathing. See, our lungs filling with air is a secondary effect; the primary movement in our breath comes from our diaphragm, that big sheet of muscle that divides our rib cage from our abdominal cavity. When the diaphragm moves down, it lengthens the space in the rib cage, causing pressure to drop around our lungs so that air rushes into the lungs to regain equilibrium. For an exhale, the reverse is true: the diaphragm moves up, space is smaller, pressure is greater, and air moves out to once again restore balance.

Many of us lose the habit of diaphragmatic breathing in adult life; stress tends to make us take shallower breaths that are led by our too-tense shoulders instead of the deeper interior muscle that can be harder to connect to. If you need help regaining a sense of your diaphragm in motion, try lying on the floor; it's harder for your shoulders to move in that position. Place your hands at the bottom of your rib cage and try to breathe in a way that moves your hands up and down. Look for motion to be centered in your abdomen rather than in your chest (but be careful not to forcefully fill your belly with air—this can slow down the healing your abdominal muscles need after pregnancy). As you advance, you'll want to expand your breathing movement to 360 degrees, seeing your back and sides expand as well. Practice breathing in this way with a slow pace; count slowly to 4 for each inhale and each exhale. Or try square breathing, where you give the same amount of time (often 4 seconds) to the inhale, the holding in of breath, the exhale, and the holding of empty lungs.

Once you've become comfortable with the pace and depth of your breath, try inviting God into the practice. One way to do this is to repeat a prayer mantra in rhythm with your respiration. Here are a few ideas to get you started; the first half is for the inhalation, the second for the exhalation.

You search me . . . you know me. (Adapted from Ps 139:1)

This is my body . . . given for you. (Luke 22:19)

As a child rests . . . so I rest in you. (Adapted from Ps 131:2)

Every tear . . . will be wiped away. (Adapted from Rev 21:4)

Take my heart . . . make it new. (Adapted from Ezek 36:26)

Be still [. . .] and know that I am God! (Ps 46:11a)

All will be well . . . all will be well. (From Julian of Norwich, *Revelations of Divine Love*)

Let everything that has breath [. . .] give praise to the LORD! (Ps 150:6)

In an ideal world, you'd be able to spend twenty solid minutes every day practicing this sort of breathing. In the actual world of a postpartum mom, try to find one or two minutes every couple of hours. In the early days of my recovery, I set an alarm on my phone for every hour on the hour; if I was busy, I dismissed the alarm, but if I could take a moment, I did. Try tying this practice to certain moments in your day, too; moments when I was sitting down to nurse or getting in the car to drive worked well for me.

This is a small practice, and it works in the fragmented moments that make up a new mom's life, but it also unites us to something much bigger. Throughout the world and throughout time, connecting with one's breath as a spiritual practice comes up again and again. The Hebrew Bible uses the same word for breath—*ruah*—as it does for the Spirit of God. Our more clinical word for breathing—respiration—has the same root word as "spirit." There is some deep wisdom in the linguistics here; God wants to draw as close to us as our own breath, and tending to our breath is a way of making space for God to do so.

A prayer to carry: God of love, be close to me as breath.

Chapter 9

Wonderfully Made

"You formed my inmost being;
   you knit me in my mother's womb.
I praise you, because I am wonderfully made;
   wonderful are your works!
   My very self you know." (Ps 139:13-14)

One of the many postpartum challenges is feeling at home again in a body that has undergone massive change. Pregnancy stretches our physical bodies past their usual limits; we are the first place the world breaks open to let a new person in, and it can leave us feeling literally broken. The physical changes that linger after pregnancy are manifold and manifest differently for everyone. For me, perineal tearing formed scar tissue that kept me in pain far longer than was normal, until I finally Googled my way into pelvic floor physical therapy. Stretched abdominal muscles and long-undiagnosed diastasis recti left my low back bearing the brunt of keeping me upright, and it constantly ached from the effort. Breastfeeding cravings were intense, almost painful, and I didn't trust my body to want good, nourishing food. Clothes didn't fit right; even as I slowly approached my pre-pregnancy weight, neither maternity clothes nor the ones I wore before were comfortable or flattering.

I knew on one level that my body had done this amazing thing of creating and nourishing an entire human life. I knew I was supposed to be grateful to it and for it in new and deepened ways. But it was (and sometimes still is) hard to shake the feeling of being a stranger in this body. It used to be mine; I hadn't loved everything about it, but I knew its quirks and mostly just . . . didn't have to think about it. Now I couldn't *stop* thinking about it, as the seasons of pregnancy and postpartum continually demanded my attention in ways I wasn't ready for. I was constantly reminded that this body that had once been mine was now shared with another person.

Learning to be grateful for my changed and changing body is an ongoing process, but one thing I have found helpful is to pray with the first half of Psalm 139. This pairs nicely with a head-to-toe acknowledgment of my body. I have this ideal of doing this while lying on my back and calling myself to an increasing awareness of my body's sensations of connection to the ground and exposure to the air, but in reality, I've only done it during a late-night nursing session and at moments when getting dressed has made me want to cry.

If you choose to pray like this, you may need to adjust this chapter for yourself. All our bodies are different, and you may not have some of the specific abilities I reference here. Please take a pen to this section as needed; mark it up and rewrite it for yourself. Go especially gently with yourself if you had a traumatic birth experience; it is very normal after such an episode to feel betrayed by your body, and it may be slow work to return to gratitude for it. Take your time—God can hold space for you while you work through it.

The opening verses of Psalm 139 read "LORD, you have probed me, you know me: / you know when I sit and stand; / you understand my thoughts from afar" (vv. 1b-2). As I remember God's deep knowledge of me, I might give thanks for my head. Its hairline is still changed by postpartum hair loss, and I still haven't learned how best to manage the coarser and wavier texture that's emerged with its regrowth. But the brain and the workings of my mind are truly marvels of God's creative power. Hormone shifts often make my thoughts feel foggy or underwater, yet I continue to learn and adapt to an entirely new way of being in the world. What a gift.

The psalm moves on to affirm that "Even before a word is on my tongue, / LORD, you know it all" (v. 4).

So I might give thanks for my mouth and for my eyes, nose, and ears. My senses open me up to the delights of this life that foreshadow the joys of heaven. They make me a stronger mother, one who picks up on my baby's cues through sight, through hearing, and even through smell. My eyes and mouth give me the power to communicate with my preverbal baby, and it is astonishing that, without trying very hard, I will give that baby the tools of speech and language. When my mouth speaks kind words and kisses my children, it passes on the very love of the God who made it.

The psalmist writes that God encircles and rests God's hand upon him (v. 5) and that God's hand guides him and holds him fast (v. 10), so I might give thanks for my arms and hands. My arms, too, hold and cradle, encircling my baby with some semblance of God's love. They tire at times, weary from the never-ending work of soothing and rocking, so I ask for God to lend me strength when I tire and to help my tiredness call me to a deeper awareness of my dependence on God. My hands are wonders of God's engineering, twenty-seven bones apiece all working in coordination to snap bodysuits, fasten diapers, and clean fresh baby skin. They learn new skills quickly and thanklessly, so often unseen by others but seen and known and loved by the God who made them.

The psalm speaks about God's ever-present spirit (v. 7), which leads me to remember my heart and lungs.

These life-giving organs operate without my input, much how God continuously sustains and protects us without our thought. I might take a moment to be grateful for the gifts of breath and pulse and to be aware of God's sustaining work in my life. I might take stock of the sturdiness of my chest, which protects the vulnerable organs inside. My breasts are there, too, and they've taken on new significance as they pass nutrition and immunity from my body to my baby's in those first vulnerable days, weeks, and months.

Psalm 139 notes that darkness cannot hide us from God (vv. 11-12), which reminds me of my abdomen, marked now by the scar tissue that developed from the deep stretch of pregnancy. This skin shelters a host of hidden, quiet organs that reside in darkness and provide me with nourishment and immunity. When my own life feels hidden and unappreciated, I might remember that God, too, gave his life over for his beloved children.

The psalm soon comes to its famous line: "You formed my inmost being; / you knit me in my mother's womb" (v. 13), and I call to mind my own womb, my uterus, my baby's first home. It has taken part now in God's ongoing work of making new life. It has stretched beyond what I could have ever thought possible, but God's imagination far exceeds mine. Returning to life after baby was painful, with cramping and bleeding, but my womb has healed and shrunken back to its normal smallness, ready—perhaps—to give life again.

The psalmist notes that even our bones are not hidden from God (v. 15), and so I consider the largest bones of my body, giving thanks for my legs and hips. They are home to solid bones and strong muscles that support my standing and walking. These legs once learned to crawl, then to walk, as my baby will do. I give thanks for my pelvic floor, too, where my body comes together, legs meeting torso and bottom and back. It has been torn and scarred but has shown such strength in carrying a human life and transitioning it into the outside world. I might say a prayer that these areas might heal fully from their postpartum woundedness.

And, finally, I remember my feet, feet that bear my weight and carry me across spaces. Feet that have swollen and deflated as my body has moved through the seasons of pregnancy and postpartum. My feet take me on adventures and stand before the most mundane of tasks. They connect me to the earth that is our home. As I consider them, I might say a prayer that I will stay grounded in God as I move through the world and through this new identity as a mother.

A prayer to carry: God, help me remember that my body is wonderfully made.

Chapter 10

Speak to the Earth

"But now ask the beasts to teach you,
    the birds of the air to tell you;
Or speak to the earth to instruct you,
    and the fish of the sea to inform you.
Which of all these does not know
    that the hand of God has done this?
In his hand is the soul of every living thing,
    and the life breath of all mortal flesh." (Job 12:7-10)

In the course of my struggles with postpartum depression, no single thing proved more healing than getting outside. You'll hear this advice often as a new mom: "Make sure you're getting out of the house!" But I don't mean just driving the neighborhood to induce a nap; I mean going really, truly outside, into fresh air and varying weather. Connecting with nature has healing benefits, and research is making it clearer that this is extraordinarily good for our mental and physical health.

It's good for our bodies and our minds to spend time outdoors. It's also good for our souls. When I struggle to see God anywhere else, God's presence is still palpable in nature. God uses creation to reach through my tiredness and to find soft spots in my hardest of hearts. The earth can teach us what it knows; it has been endowed with a wisdom by the God who made it and who is still making us.

When you think of nature, you might think first of vast landscapes removed from human development: deep, quiet woods; rocky, mountainous vistas; wild, wonderful seas. For many of us, these places take some effort to get to, so they're a rare treat saved for full-blown vacation time. This is even more true with a baby, especially since baby gear makes packing for a day's outing look like you're moving house. The practicalities are harder: you'll be communing with nature from behind a stroller or baby carrier or whatever other contraption makes this tenable for you. You'll listen for birdsong over the coos or wails of your own offspring. You might be pinched or scratched in the face as you strive to put your senses to work. So the large-scale outdoor getaways might be out of reach for now.

But bits of nature are waiting for us everywhere, patchworked throughout even our big cities: parks, backyards, flowerpots, and, most important for me, bird feeders. I started birding when my oldest was about eighteen months old, and now I spend outside time listening for birdsong and wrestling my binoculars away from a toddler so I can observe whatever feathered beauties cross my path. Birding has taught me how to pay attention better; once I started looking for birds, it was astonishing to realize that this beauty had been there, unobserved by me, all along.

God is present not only in the big things of nature but also in the small ones. The incredible biodiversity of the tiniest plants and animals speaks of God's endless creativity. Dandelions growing in sidewalk cracks give witness to God's stubbornness in trying to get to us. God is present in window-box gardens and city park habitat—anywhere that life and breath are evident. Scott Sampson reminds me of this in his book *How to Raise a Wild Child: The Art and Science of Falling in Love with Nature.* This book posits that nature connection is vital for our kids; I'm making the claim that it's vital for us mothers, too.

Dr. Sampson encourages parents to remember that, to a child, even a single anthill or mud puddle is full of wonder. I've learned to find wonder there, too, especially when I don't have the time or energy for elaborate outings. Nature becomes big and beautiful again when we try to experience it from a child's view. We can get down to a lower level by lying in the grass, letting our fingers feel different textures, looking up at the sky in all its depth and endless variety. Feeling small in this way is good for us. It is different from the smallness that we often feel in our motherhood. It helps us order ourselves rightly within something much bigger than ourselves.

When we become mothers, we're arguably more deeply connected to nature than we were before. We've now participated in the great biological dance of perpetuating the species. We've been through pregnancy and birth and (perhaps) breastfeeding, joining all our mammalian sisters in nourishing our young by giving over our very bodies as shelter and food. Nature teaches us something about God, who also gives over self in order to nourish and protect us.

I love this idea of being taught by the plants and animals, the very creatures whose care we were charged with at creation. Our relationship with them is not meant to be one of power or of dominance or of benefits flowing in only one direction. It's, rather, a symbiotic relationship we're meant to have with them, one of giving and taking, teaching and listening. Nature preaches to us if we let it. Its very presence testifies to the abundant love and bountiful creativity of the God who loves us into being and who sustains all creation with love.

A prayer to carry: Creator God, help me find you in all you have made.

Chapter 11

Give You Rest

"Come to me, all you who labor and are burdened, and I will give you rest. Take my yoke upon you and learn from me, for I am meek and humble of heart; and you will find rest for yourselves. For my yoke is easy, and my burden light." (Matt 11:28-30)

Remember the uninterrupted sleep of your prebaby days? Going to bed when you got tired and sleeping right on through the night? Sometimes even staying in bed after you woke up? For most of us with children, that kind of rest is now a sweet memory, a once-reliable part of our lives that has been forever altered by having a baby. No more are the luxurious lie-ins, the spontaneous weekend naps. Rest feels elusive, leaving us scrambling after it. It is subject to disruption, both direct and indirect, as conflicting advice about sleep safety and sleep training may turn your family's rest into an area of tension. Sleep has turned stressful.

"[L]earn from me," Jesus says as he promises rest (Matt 11:29). This is perhaps not very promising to hear from one whose attempts to withdraw were met by needy crowds (see Mark 6:33), crowds to whose needs he responded freely and generously. This is a man who ministered madly for three years, whipped up a frenzied following, and finished it up with a death that was not even the final rest it usually is. If Jesus is here to teach us about rest, we might be in trouble.

But even if we don't think of rest as characterizing Jesus's ministry, when we look closely, he does make time for it. He begins his ministry with something like a retreat, withdrawing into the desert for uninterrupted prayer. The gospels often show him in private prayer. He withdraws from crowds, enjoying the company of those closest to him. He even curls up on a cushion while traveling by boat with his disciples, falling into a sleep so deep that they need to rouse him so he doesn't miss the storm that seems like it could be the end of them all.

He also instructs his disciples to rest; after missions of preaching and healing, he calls them away for restful solitude (see Mark 6:31). In doing so, he echoes the commands of God in the Old Testament that set aside an entire day of the week for rest and worship. God did not make us for endless toil; your need for rest is not a sign of weakness or because you don't love your baby enough. This is part of how you were made, for a rhythm of work and rest, and it is a very real need.

Unfortunately, your baby doesn't know this, and there is or has been or will be a time when their needs and rhythms seem to be in conflict with your own. And your needs will, for a time, take a back seat, because sometimes that's what parenting is. But they can't be set aside indefinitely, and tending to them even imperfectly can make a world of difference in our mental health as moms.

But our rest time now feels scarce and precious and consequently comes with an odd pressure. It can feel as if all our own needs come flooding in, competing even with each other. Do I shower or sleep? Eat or sleep? Catch up with that friend I've been neglecting . . . or sleep? Should I catch up on laundry? Pray? Exercise? Do a hobby that will exercise intellectual and creative muscles in danger of withering from disuse?

Our own needs for rest can seem to conflict with each other because there are different kinds of restorative rest, and they're all good and important. There is full, deep, uninterrupted sleep. There are hobbies and leisure activities that help restore our hearts. There is restorative alone time for introverts and therapeutic social time for extroverts. The desire is to maximize the time, to ensure we get the most benefit in stress reduction and energy renewal. Even our breaks can fall into the trap of trying to be productive.

Which is why it's important that Jesus tells us *why* we should learn from him here: "I am meek and humble of heart" (Matt 11:29). Our aspirations for our breaks will often go unmet. As in every area of our lives, we need to adjust our expectations. Rest and breaks will come in fits and starts; they are forever interruptible.

Our rest may remain incomplete for now, never attaining us the energy we had in our prebaby days. But Jesus reminds us where our fullest rest is to be found when he beckons, "Come to me" (Matt 11:28). Our true rest is with him, in his arms, in his heart. We can find our way there without long periods of intensely focused prayer; we can rest in him in whatever else we're doing. We can come to Jesus in our napping, invite him into whatever gives us solace and refreshment, remember that he's already there in anything that renews or heals us. Because he is here with us, Emmanuel dwelling with us. He knows the weariness of the human condition. And he calls us to come sit with him and rest a while.

A prayer to carry: Jesus, let me rest in you.

Closing Benediction

All Things New

"I heard a loud voice from the throne saying, 'Behold, God's dwelling is with the human race. He will dwell with them and they will be his people and God himself will always be with them [as their God]. He will wipe every tear from their eyes, and there shall be no more death or mourning, wailing or pain, [for] the old order has passed away.' The one who sat on the throne said, 'Behold, I make all things new.' " (Rev 21:3-5a)

For me, finding my way into motherhood has been a long, convoluted road. Progress through my pain was never as linear as I would have chosen. There were better days and worse days, improvements and relapses. There were moments of hope and energy, followed all too quickly by moments of anguish and despair. In some ways, I'm still recovering. I still grieve the loss of what I thought those early months and years should have been.

When I get mad at my kids (a very normal part of parenting, I am told), I have an added layer of guilt, wondering if I failed to bond with them in the way I should have. Postpartum depression left scars on my heart that are still very real. I don't know what the future holds, of course, but it feels pretty possible that this experience has permanently changed me, and not always for the better.

But I also have an oddly distinct memory of a day I turned a significant corner in my own recovery. This was an important day for me, but it isn't a very good story. It was a day when nothing in particular happened. I nursed the baby. I got breakfast for the toddler. I drank the tea my husband made me. I swept up cereal. I cleaned the sink. It was time to nurse again. Everything was the same, but it was also different. Throughout my postpartum struggles, I'd had many days where I could muster up some semblance of gratitude and dutiful Christian joy. But this day brought a simple, easy cheerfulness, a default happiness, a core knowledge that my life was, in fact, good. That was it. That's the whole story.

This day was my third on a hormone supplement that my doctor prescribed. In the months after starting this supplement, I still had hard moments. But I didn't feel overwhelmed by my feelings in the same way, and I was more able to regain control of my irritability and sadness. With a little more time, my energy came back, too. It was still an exhausting and overwhelming life at times, but I was more prepared to meet it.

There was a strange tension here: on the one hand, this mood felt foreign after my months of feeling down. But it also slipped back into my life so easily I could have almost not noticed it. It felt like a homecoming, and not an overtly emotional one. Home is, after all, a place often taken for granted. It's not exciting; it's just good. Returning after being away carries a subtle joy, an easing of travel tension, an ability to breathe. That's what this was. I was, finally, coming home to myself.

And it's only gotten better. As I write this, I'm several more years and another baby in. My third postpartum experience has been everything I ever dreamed. I am wildly in love with my baby—with all my kids—and am finding so much joy in being their mom. It's a complicated joy at times, and I am so far from perfect, but I keep becoming more able to see God, who keeps showing up amid all my failings. I have reconnected with the person I was unable to be for a while. I know how to have fun again; I enjoy the things I enjoy. I am able to witness to God's work of making new, to answer God's call to "behold." I wonder at the ever-newness of our God and know that this work of renewal is, as Revelation puts it, "trustworthy and true" (21:5b).

Every so often in this life, we get these clear moments of renewal and healing—moments when God's presence is clear and radiant, though God was never not with us in the suffering. These moments are full of joy and hope, but they are just a shadow of when the pain will pass away once and for all. Even when we are whole again, as healed as we ever will be, there are hard days. This life is broken by sin and suffering, and parenting comes with its fair share. There are plenty of interrupted nights and toddler behaviors ahead. There are school stresses and teenage hormones on the horizon. We have taken on the astoundingly humble work of ushering a new person into the world, and there's no way it will be easy.

So the hope here is not to never struggle or suffer, at least not in this life. It's to be able to respond to the struggles from a place of trust. To see abundance where resources (including our own energy and love) appear scarce. To operate out of a generosity that only comes when we trust in our God to renew us as we go.

Because God does. God makes all things new. Even me. Even you. God has the power to end all death and mourning and pain, and God promises to do so. In the meantime, God acknowledges our suffering and sits with us in it. God, the maker of heaven and earth, the one who sustains all things in love, promises to wipe every tear from your eyes. *Every* tear. Each tear and sigh and sorrow is seen and known by the one who made your heart. Your pain is held closely by the one who dwells here, with us.

A prayer to carry: God, wipe away my tears, and make me new in you.

Appendix A

Lectio Divina for Moms

This book came out of the practice of *Lectio Divina*—or, at least, prayer inspired by the practice. *Lectio Divina* is a method of prayer that takes as its starting point the belief that Scripture is not just a static set of words on a page but, rather, is the *living* Word of a God who remains with us and speaks to our lives as they are here and now. It takes up a posture of listening to the God who still speaks in the words of Scripture.

Lectio Divina traditionally consists of four movements: reading (*lectio*), meditation (*meditatio*), prayer (*oratio*), and contemplation (*contemplatio*). This is distinct from studying or analyzing the text, although that practice, too, can be fruitful for our prayer. *Lectio Divina*, rather, invites the practitioner to enter more and more deeply into the text and to encounter God there.

This is most often a monastic practice, performed primarily by those who have committed to celibacy and for whom this prayer is part of their primary work. They have significant time dedicated to it in their daily schedule. They are able to engage with the texts deeply and intentionally, wrestling with God and taking the fruits of their prayer periods into their other work.

For a mother who wants to pray with Scripture in this way, it will, of course, look a little different. It might involve very short passages, even shorter than you're thinking (see Appendix B for some suggestions). It will undoubtedly involve interruption. The four movements are unlikely to occur in a single sitting but might, rather, be spread out over a day or week—and they might not be distinct or recognizable at all.

Maybe it's even a stretch to call this practice *Lectio Divina*. But taking the time to sit with God's Word does bear fruit, even if it's not immediately obvious. It is a means of putting ourselves into contact with Jesus himself, who is, after all, the Word of God.

Appendix B

Briefer Scriptures for Overwhelming Times

The reflections in this book are intentionally brief, designed to be consumable by a distracted brain within a single feeding session. Some days, even they might be too much, so I've gathered here even shorter snippets from the Scripture passages we've considered.

These are meant as a bonus gift for you, and I hope you'll find creative ways to use them. They are easy to memorize and can be repeated as mantras. Write them in your planner, scribble them on sticky notes, put them up where you'll see them. Have a trusted friend write them on diapers for a late-night reminder that you are not alone.

If you've been able to read the reflections, I hope they can serve as reminders of what is there. If you haven't yet, consider them an invitation to at least encounter the loving, living Word of God in words far more important than mine.

[W]e also groan within ourselves as we wait for adoption. (Rom 8:23)

I will give you a new heart. (Ezek 36:26)

Wait for God. (Ps 42:6)

[S]he, from her poverty, has contributed all she had. (Mark 12:44)

Woman, why are you weeping? (John 20:15)

[A]nd you yourself a sword will pierce. (Luke 2:35)

[T]ake the child and his mother. (Matt 2:13)

Let everything that has breath / give praise to the LORD! *(Ps 150:6)*

I praise you, because I am wonderfully made. (Ps 139:14)

In his hand is the soul of every living thing. (Job 12:10)

Come to me . . . and I will give you rest. (Matt 11:28)

Behold, I make all things new. (Rev 21:5)

Appendix C

A Litany of Saints for Postpartum Struggles

When I struggled with postpartum depression, I wished often that the church offered an official patron saint for this disorder. Since it does not, I've gathered up a few saints who might understand the trials of this season of life. Most of these are mothers, and some struggled with their mental health. I hope you might find a companion here who can walk with you through the trials of this time. If none of these speak to you in particular, praying through this list as a litany and calling on this whole cloud of saintly companions might be a helpful prayer practice.

We've already reflected on Mary of Nazareth, especially under her title as Sorrowful Mother. Even the

Mother of God was not spared from the trials and sorrows of motherhood—indeed, hers were harsher than most. Mary reminds us that holiness is not always accompanied by happiness, at least not in this life. She hears us with compassion in all the joys and sorrows of finding our way into motherhood. Mary, Sorrowful Mother, pray for us!

Elizabeth, relative of Mary and mother of John the Baptist, is another biblical woman whose motherhood came with bewildering signs. While she was the recipient of a joyful miracle, a baby who should not have come in her old age, her pregnancy would have been all the more challenging because of her maturity. In addition, her husband had gone mute and her cousin turned up with even more miraculous news; there is much cause for concern here. Like Mary, she found God present in these surprises, letting confusion turn to wonder. St. Elizabeth, pray for us!

Mary Magdalene was not a mother, as far as we know, but she is remembered for staying close to Jesus even in her sorrow. When she felt sure he was gone for good, she remained close to him, leaving her ready to be the first to receive the news of the resurrection. May we, too, remain near to Jesus in our struggles and keep our hearts ready for the joy he promises, whenever it may come. St. Mary Magdalene, pray for us!

Monica of Hippo (331–87) is a mom who shed many tears over her son, whose behaviors and beliefs as a young adult caused her great distress. The trials of her motherhood extended far beyond its early years, but she never gave up trusting in God. Her persistence was eventually rewarded, and she got to see her son's conversion—we know him now as St. Augustine. Monica models for us a persistent, even stubborn, faith in God for ourselves and our children. St. Monica, pray for us!

Dymphna (seventh century) was the daughter of a pagan Irish king and a Christian mother. Her life was one of tragic abuse by her father that led ultimately to his murder of her as a teenager. A tradition soon emerged that claimed healing of mental illness for those who visited her tomb. This led to her patronage of all who suffer from mental health disorders, and since postpartum mood disorders are a subset of those, we will claim her here. St. Dymphna, pray for us!

Rita of Cascia (1381–1457) makes our list because she is often named as the patron saint of heartbroken women. Her own life was one of deep tragedy; her parents forced her into a marriage she did not want, and she endured years of abuse until her husband's death. She became an Augustinian nun and lived the rest of her life in prayer and service, reminding us that whatever heartbreak we endure is not the end of our story and is not the end of God's dealings with us. St. Rita of Cascia, pray for us!

Elizabeth Ann Seton (1774–1821) was a mother of five who had to find her way through motherhood after losing her husband to illness. She found the inner resources to support her children, and she found God in the Catholic Church, to which she converted in 1805. When her children were grown, she established a reli-

gious order and a school that is credited as a forerun-
ner of the Catholic school system in the United States.
St. Elizabeth Ann Seton, pray for us!

Zélie Martin (1831–77) was the mother of five
daughters who dedicated their lives to God as nuns.
Zélie was a mother who knew the trials of parenting. Letters she wrote during her lifetime recount her
frustration at her children's obstinance and worries
for their future—even that of the child who would
become St. Thérèse of Lisieux. Zélie reminds us that
raising saints is hard work and that the struggles are
not the end of the story. St. Zélie Martin, pray for us!

Rose Hawthorne Lathrop (1851–1926) was a mother
who suffered from postpartum depression and psycho-
sis; her case was severe enough that she needed to be
separated from her infant son for several months while
she recovered. She did recover, but her suffering was
not over—she later lost her son to diphtheria and her
husband to alcoholism. Her pain was not the end of her
story, though; she went on to care for cancer patients

living in poverty and is now on the church's path to sainthood. Servant of God Rose Hawthorne Lathrop, pray for us!

Gianna Beretta Molla (1922–62) was an Italian physician and the mother of four. She is best known for refusing medical treatment that would have terminated her fourth pregnancy and ultimately dying due to complications from that pregnancy and delivery. But it was not just her death that makes her a saint; she lived her entire life in love for God and her family. Her letters to her husband, many of which are simply reminders of the ordinary tasks of their shared life, are imbued with this love. St. Gianna Beretta Molla, pray for us!

Appendix D

Other Resources

In the introduction to this book, I mentioned that its intent is to support but not replace the expertise of medical and mental health professionals, especially in the case of postpartum mood disorders. Mothers often believe they should not need care, but you deserve to feel better, and you may need support getting there. If you need help connecting to these resources, here are some places to start.

First and foremost, if you think you may hurt yourself or your baby, this is a mental health emergency, not a moral failing. In the United States, do not hesitate to call or text 911 or the Suicide and Crisis Lifeline at 988. You can also visit your local emergency room for assistance.

If you and your child are not in immediate danger, your existing team of medical professionals can help you. Your primary care provider, your obstetrician, or your child's pediatrician can all provide or help connect you to the care you need. If you have an established relationship with a therapist, you can also reach out to them; if not, one of these other doctors can make a referral. You can also search for a therapist at https://www.psychologytoday.com/.

You can learn more about postpartum mood disorders from Postpartum Support International (https://www.postpartum.net). Their online provider directory lists mental health professionals who have completed specialized training in perinatal mental health (https://psidirectory.com). They also provide a helpline specific to maternal mental health at 1-800-944-4773.

The book *This Isn't What I Expected: Overcoming Postpartum Depression* by Karen Kleiman and Valerie Raskin was hugely helpful to me in unraveling this disorder from a clinical perspective. Karen Kleiman also founded the Postpartum Stress Center, whose online presence at https://www.postpartumstress.com has more resources for mothers who are struggling.

In chapter 4, I mention Naomi Stadlen's book *What Mothers Do: Especially When It Looks Like Nothing*. This book's gentle affirmation of the work I was doing as a mother was absolutely invaluable.

If you've reached the PBS KIDS years of parenting, you might be familiar with Dr. Scott Sampson, the paleontologist who appears at the end of each episode of *Dinosaur Train*. His book *How to Raise a Wild Child: The Art and Science of Falling in Love with Nature* happened to be the first thing I read after my second child was born. It is specifically about getting kids out into nature, which is not the only important thing about parenting but which gave me hope to see past the overwhelming demands of our day-to-day realities and start to dream about what I actually wanted our family life to look like.

Other parenting books that have provide reassurance and hope include *How to Talk So Little Kids Will Listen* by Joanna Faber and Julie King and anything cowritten by Daniel J. Siegel and Tina Payne Bryson, starting with *The Whole-Brain Child*.